anythink

Smithsonian

LITTLE EXPLORER

ASTRONAUT
IN TRAINING

by Kathryn Clay

CAPSTONE PRESS
a capstone imprint

Little Explorer is published by Capstone Press,
1710 Roe Crest Drive, North Mankato, Minnesota 56003

www.mycapstone.com

Library of Congress Cataloging-in-Publication Data
Names: Clay, Kathryn, author.
Title: Astronaut in training / by Kathryn Clay.
Description: North Mankato, Minnesota : Capstone Press, [2017]
| Series: Smithsonian little explorer. Little astronauts. |
Audience: Ages 7-9. | Audience: K to grade 3. | Includes
bibliographical references and index.
Identifiers: LCCN 2016043032| ISBN 9781515736608
(library binding) | ISBN 9781515736745 (pbk.) |
ISBN 9781515736783 (ebook (pdf))
Subjects: LCSH: Astronauts—Juvenile literature. | Outer space—
Exploration—Juvenile literature.
Classification: LCC TL793 .C6264 2017 | DDC 629.45/07—dc23
LC record available at https://lccn.loc.gov/2016043032

Editorial Credits
Arnold Ringstad, editor; Jake Nordby, designer and
production specialist

Our very special thanks to Dr. Valerie Neal, Curator and Chair
of the Space History Department at the Smithsonian National
Air and Space Museum for her curatorial review. Capstone
would also like to thank Kealy Gordon, Smithsonian Institution
Product Development Manager, and the following at Smithsonian
Enterprises: Christopher A. Liedel, President; Carol LeBlanc,
Senior Vice President; Brigid Ferraro, Vice President; Ellen
Nanney, Licensing Manager.

Photo Credits
Alamy: NASA Photo, 20; AP Images: Rex Features/ESA-V. Crobu,
9; Dreamstime: Paul Hakimata, 10; Glow images: SuperStock, 1;
NASA, 3, 4, 5 (middle), 5 (right), 8, 11 (top), 11 (bottom), 12 (top),
12 (bottom), 14, 15, 16, 17 (bottom right), 18–19, 21, 23, 24–25, 27
(top), 27 (bottom), 28–29, 30–31, Houston Chronicle, Smiley N.
Pool, cover, B. Stafford, 12–13, Benny Benavides, 28, Bill Ingalls,
19, Joel Kowsky, 22; Newscom: Blend Images/Hill Street Studios,
6 (left); Science Source: Allen Green, 17 (top right), Publiphoto,
26, RIA Novosti, 5 (left); Shutterstock: Kolo, 17, LOVEgraphic, 24,
MarcelClemens, 32, pio3, 27 (background)

Design Elements: Shutterstock Images: Ovchinnkov Vladimir,
Shay Yacobinski, Teneresa

Printed in the United States of America.
010053S17

TABLE OF CONTENTS

WHO ARE ASTRONAUTS? 4

BECOMING AN ASTRONAUT 6

BASIC TRAINING 8

ADVANCED TRAINING 10

PREPARING FOR SPACEWALKS 12

WEIGHTLESSNESS 14

PRACTICING WITH MODELS 16

THE SOYUZ SPACECRAFT 18

SPACE GEAR 20

MISSION TRAINING 22

TRAINING WITH MISSION CONTROL 24

THE FUTURE OF ASTRONAUT TRAINING 26

A TOUGH AND REWARDING JOB 28

GLOSSARY 30

CRITICAL THINKING USING
THE COMMON CORE 31

READ MORE 31

INTERNET SITES 31

INDEX 32

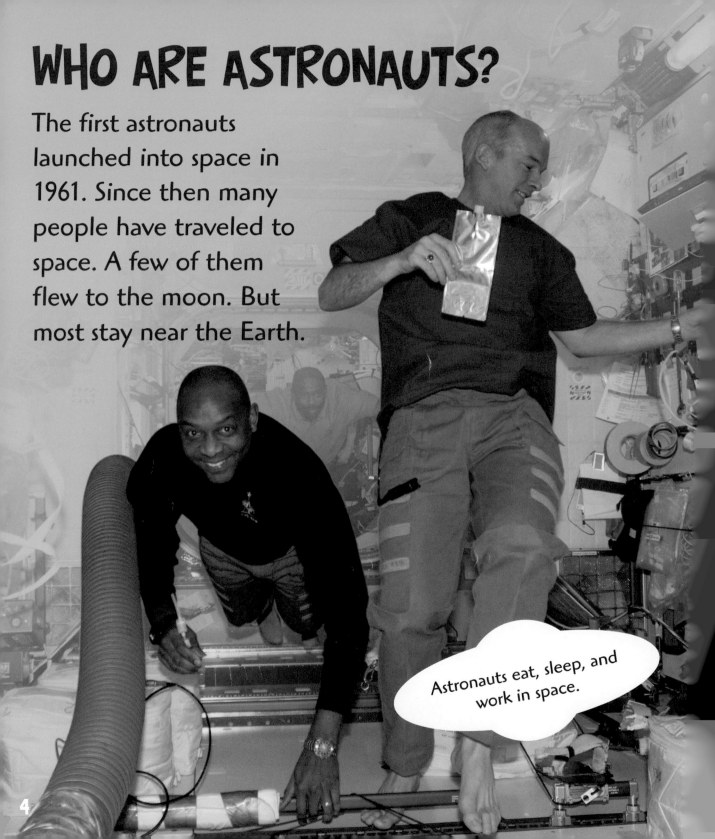

WHO ARE ASTRONAUTS?

The first astronauts launched into space in 1961. Since then many people have traveled to space. A few of them flew to the moon. But most stay near the Earth.

Astronauts eat, sleep, and work in space.

4

Neil Armstrong

Yuri Gagarin

Tim Peake

FAMOUS ASTRONAUTS

name	country	first mission	previous job
Yuri Gagarin	Soviet Union	1961	military pilot
Valentina Tereshkova	Soviet Union	1963	skydiver/factory worker
Neil Armstrong	United States	1966	test pilot/engineer
Sally Ride	United States	1983	physicist
Chris Hadfield	Canada	1995	military pilot/engineer
Tim Peake	United Kingdom	2015	military pilot

Early astronauts were pilots. Most were in the military. Today other kinds of people can be astronauts too. Many are scientists. Some are engineers. All astronauts face tough training.

BECOMING AN ASTRONAUT

Becoming an astronaut is competitive. A college degree is a must. Future astronauts study science and engineering. The space agency NASA chooses and trains U.S. astronauts.

Astronauts must be healthy and physically fit. They need excellent eyesight. They face a difficult interview process.

Students who want to become astronauts must study hard in school.

U.S. ASTRONAUT REQUIREMENTS

These are just a few of the many requirements for becoming a NASA astronaut.

☐ height between 62 and 75 inches (157–191 centimeters)

☐ blood pressure 140/90 or lower

☐ three years of professional experience after earning a college degree, or 1,000 hours of experience flying jets

☐ swimming test, showing astronauts can survive if their spacecraft lands in water

BASIC TRAINING

U.S. astronauts train in Houston, Texas. Astronauts from other nations train in their home countries and in the United States. They spend years preparing. They learn the skills they need for space missions.

Astronauts have trained at the Johnson Space Center in Houston since the 1960s.

Survival skills are important too. A spacecraft could land in a remote area. Astronauts learn how to treat injuries. They learn how to build shelters and find clean water.

Astronauts Tim Peake (right) and Samantha Cristoforetti prepare dinner over a fire during survival training.

Training for a space mission is a long process. Italian Astronaut Roberto Vittori explains that the training feels like a journey itself. He says, "In some ways, our space flight is as much the end of a long journey as it is the beginning of a new one."

ADVANCED TRAINING

Many astronauts study the International Space Station (ISS). It will be their home in space. They learn about its different parts and rooms. Full-sized models let them practice moving through the ISS.

A huge space station model is located in Houston.

Astronauts work with Russian cosmonauts. They learn the Russian language and customs. The cosmonauts learn English. They all train together in Houston and Star City, Russia.

An astronaut (top) and cosmonaut (bottom) train together in Star City.

THE INTERNATIONAL SPACE STATION

The ISS is a science lab in space! Countries around the world worked together to build it. The ISS circles Earth every 90 minutes. By 2016 more than 200 people from 18 countries had visited it.

PREPARING FOR SPACEWALKS

Astronauts sometimes leave their spacecraft. This is called a spacewalk. Spacewalk training is done underwater. Astronauts can float and move like they will in space.

UNDERWATER

IN SPACE

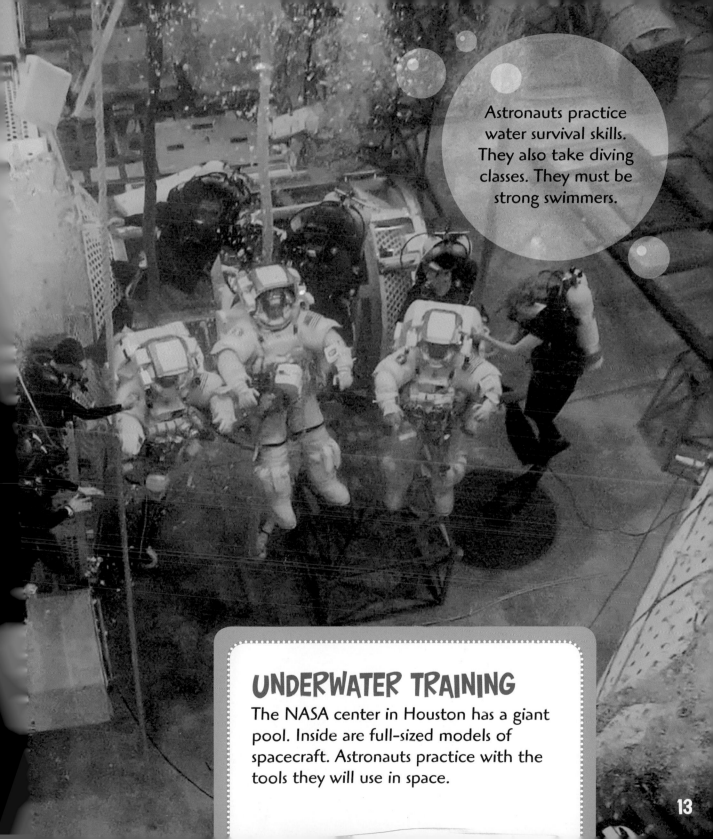

Astronauts practice water survival skills. They also take diving classes. They must be strong swimmers.

UNDERWATER TRAINING

The NASA center in Houston has a giant pool. Inside are full-sized models of spacecraft. Astronauts practice with the tools they will use in space.

13

WEIGHTLESSNESS

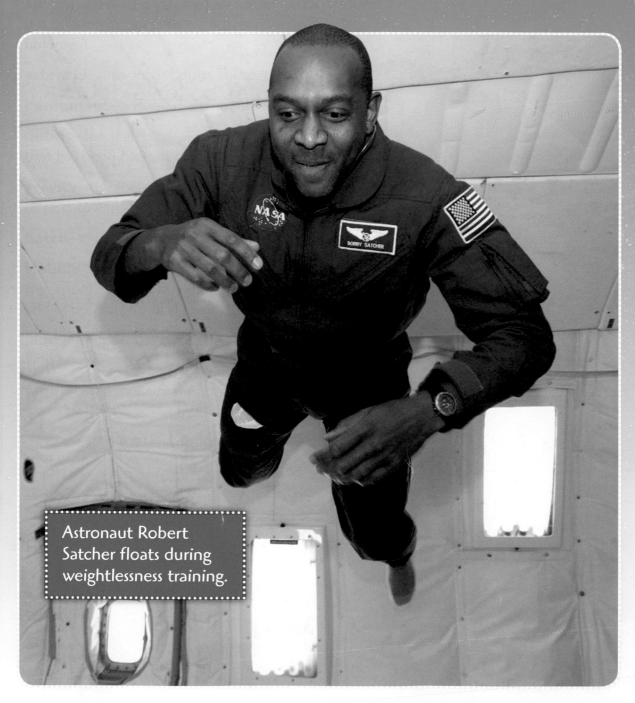

Astronaut Robert Satcher floats during weightlessness training.

Astronauts train for weightlessness, or floating in space. They ride in airplanes that fly in large upside-down U shapes. Passengers feel weightless and float around for about 25 seconds. The plane does this up to 60 times during one flight.

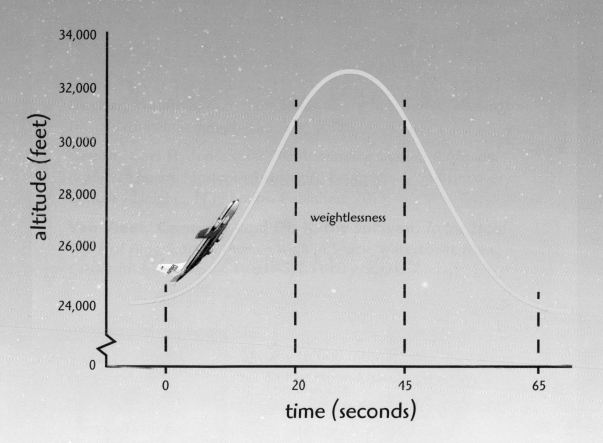

This training makes many people experience motion sickness. The airplanes are nicknamed "vomit comets."

PRACTICING WITH MODELS

The main U.S. spacecraft from 1981 to 2011 was the space shuttle. It looked like a jet airplane. Shuttle training happened in Houston.

space shuttle

Astronauts trained using full-sized models of the space shuttle. Models could tilt upward to practice launches. They could tilt downward to practice landings. Space shuttle astronauts spent more than 300 hours in the model before a flight.

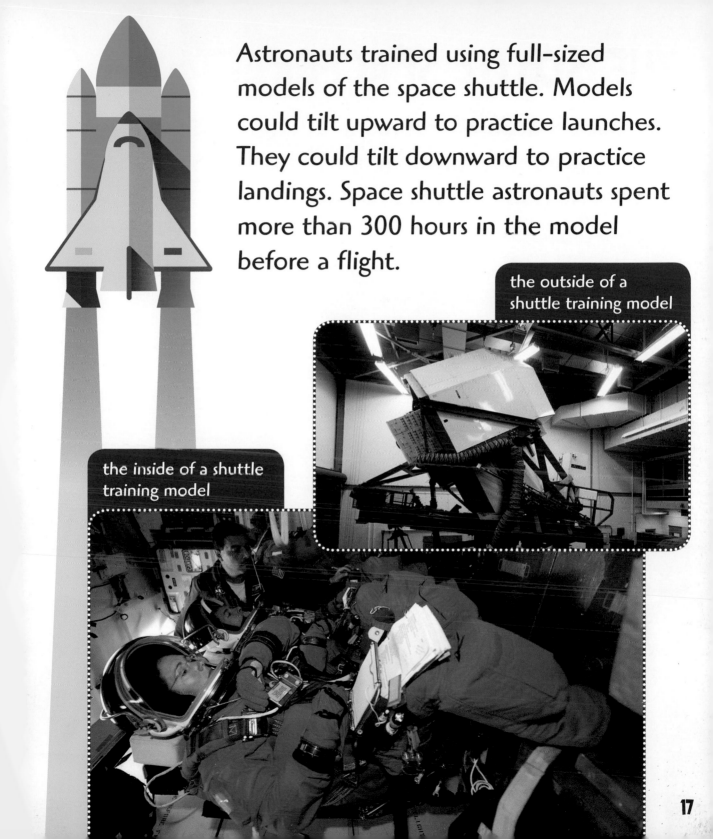

the outside of a shuttle training model

the inside of a shuttle training model

THE SOYUZ SPACECRAFT

The space shuttle was retired in 2011. Now all astronauts travel in small Russian spacecraft. These are called Soyuz. In English, *Soyuz* means "union." Each spacecraft holds three people.

supply spacecraft

a Soyuz spacecraft attached to the International Space Station

Astronauts practice in a Soyuz model. The model is in Russia.

SPACE GEAR

Wearing a space suit is no easy task. The suits are bulky to keep astronauts safe. Putting on a suit can take about 45 minutes!

Astronauts must be comfortable in their suits before missions. They learn how to put on each piece. Then they practice moving and working in the suits. Each task is practiced many times before a mission.

Astronaut Victor Glover gets help putting on his space suit in training.

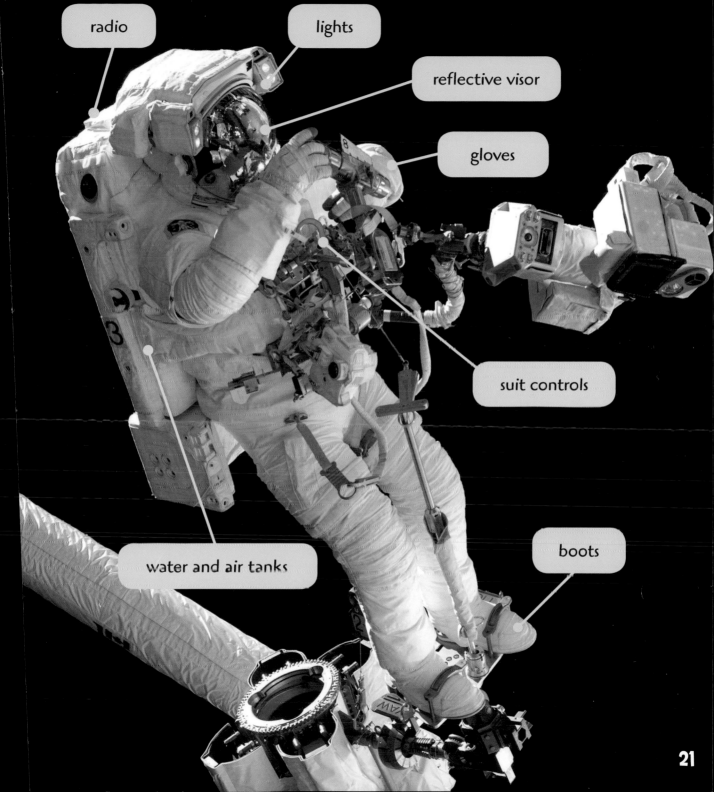

radio

lights

reflective visor

gloves

suit controls

water and air tanks

boots

MISSION TRAINING

Astronauts are assigned to different missions.
Mission training can take up to three years.
Astronauts learn details about their missions.
Each astronaut has a special job.

A crew stands in front of their rocket before a mission.

Everyone learns the skills they need. Some may build or repair parts of the space station. Others may work on science experiments. The crew trains together. They practice working as a team.

A crew goes over the plans for an upcoming mission.

TRAINING WITH MISSION CONTROL

Mission control supports the astronauts. Workers there are called flight controllers. Astronauts and flight controllers practice their missions together.

The U.S. mission control center is in Houston. The European center is in Darmstadt, Germany. The Russian center is in Korolev, Russia.

Darmstadt, Germany

Korolev, Russia

Houston, Texas

Flight controllers try to think of any problems that might happen. Solving problems on the ground prepares them for success.

Flight controllers can see information about the spacecraft. They pass along this information to the crew. They work to keep the crew safe.

THE FUTURE OF ASTRONAUT TRAINING

Astronauts traveled to the moon in the 1960s and 1970s. They have not traveled to other planets yet. But that may soon change. Today's astronauts are training for the missions of the future.

The astronauts of tomorrow may explore Mars.

Orion
crew module

Orion service module
(holds engines and supplies)

The United States is building a new type of spacecraft called Orion. It will travel far into space. Astronauts might even land on Mars. The mission will bring many challenges. Astronauts study these challenges on the ISS.

inside an Orion spacecraft during training

A TOUGH AND REWARDING JOB

Training for space travel isn't easy. Astronauts push their minds and bodies to the limit. They risk their lives on dangerous missions.

However astronauts say the hard work is worth it. They get to see Earth from space. They do important scientific work. And they work alongside other space travelers. All this is made possible by the astronauts' intense training.

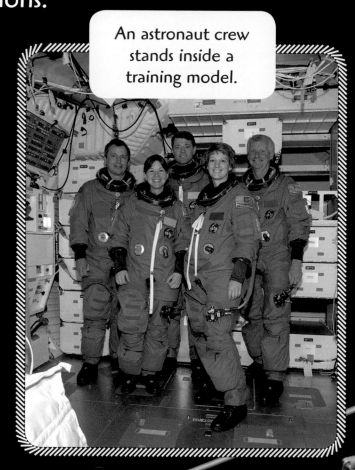

An astronaut crew stands inside a training model.

Astronaut John Grunsfeld gives a thumbs-up in space.

GLOSSARY

blood pressure—the force of blood as it flows through a person's body

competitive—involving many different people struggling to win or succeed

cosmonaut—a Russian astronaut

custom—a tradition in a culture or society

engineer—a person who designs, builds, and improves things

intense—difficult and requiring a lot of energy and effort

model—something that is made to look like a person, animal, or object

pilot—a person who flies airplanes

remote—far from other things

spacecraft—a craft built to travel in space

weightlessness—the feeling of not being pulled down toward Earth

CRITICAL THINKING USING THE COMMON CORE

1. How do astronauts train for spacewalks? Where do they do this training? (Key Ideas and Details)

2. Astronauts must be very healthy. Why is it important for people who fly into space to be healthy? (Integration of Knowledge and Ideas)

3. Page 17 shows the inside and outside of a spacecraft model used for training. How does seeing both the inside and outside help you understand how this training tool works? (Integration of Knowledge and Ideas)

READ MORE

Bredeson, Carmen, and Marianne Dyson. *Astronauts Explore the Galaxy.* Launch Into Space! New York: Enslow Publishing, 2015.

Chastain, Zachary. *Becoming an Astronaut.* Kid's Library of Space Exploration. Vestal, N.Y.,: Village Earth Press, 2014.

Hayden, Kate. *Astronaut: Living in Space.* New York: DK Publishing, 2012.

INTERNET SITES

FactHound offers a safe, fun way to find Internet sites related to this book. All of the sites on FactHound have been researched by our staff.

Here's all you do:

Visit www.facthound.com

Type in this code: 9781515736608

Check out projects, games and lots more at
www.capstonekids.com

INDEX

Armstrong, Neil, 5

college, 6, 7
cosmonauts, 11

engineers, 5

Gagarin, Yuri, 5

Hadfield, Chris, 5
health, 6, 7
Houston, Texas, 8, 11, 13, 16

International Space Station, 10, 11, 27

Mars, 27
mission control, 24, 25
models, 17, 19
moon, 4, 26

Orion spacecraft, 27

Peake, Tim, 5
pilots, 5

Ride, Sally, 5

scientists, 5
Soyuz spacecraft, 18, 19
space shuttle, 16, 17, 18
space suits, 20, 21
spacewalks, 12
Star City, Russia, 11
survival skills, 9, 13

Tereshkova, Valentina, 5

underwater training, 12, 13

Vittori, Roberto, 9